Properties of Materials

Hot or Cold

Charlotte Guillain

www.heinemannlibrary.co.uk
Visit our website to find out more information about Heinemann Library books.

To order:

☎ Phone +44 (0) 1865 888066
📄 Fax +44 (0) 1865 314091
💻 Visit www.heinemannlibrary.co.uk

Heinemann is an imprint of Capstone Global Library Limited, a company incorporated in England and Wales having its registered office at 7 Pilgrim Street, London, EC4V 6LB – Registered company number: 6695582

"Heinemann" is a registered trademark of Pearson Education Limited, under licence to Capstone Global Library Limited

Edited by Charlotte Guillain and Catherine Veitch
Designed by Joanna Hinton-Malivoire
Picture research by Elizabeth Alexander
Originated by Heinemann Library
Printed by South China Printing Company Limited

ISBN 978 0 431 19346 5 (hardback)
13 12 11 10 09
10 9 8 7 6 5 4 3 2 1

British Library Cataloguing in Publication Data
Guillain, Charlotte
Hot or cold. – (Properties of materials)
536
A full catalogue record for this book is available from the British Library.

Acknowledgements
The author and publishers are grateful to the following for permission to reproduce copyright material: Alamy pp. **10** (© Aflo Foto Agency), **12** (© Imagestate Media Partners Limited – Impact Photos), **13** (© Tim Gainey), **16** (© Bon Appetit), **19** (© Chris Rout), **21** (© Paul Felix Photography); © Capstone Publishers p. **22** (Karon Dubke); Corbis pp. **9** (© José Fuste Raga/zefa), **14** (© Charles O'Rear); © Corbis p. **17**; iStockphoto p. **6** (© Jon Schulte); Photolibrary p. **18** (Beau Lark/Fancy); Shutterstock pp. **4** (© Thomas Nord), **5** (© Liv Friis-Larsen), **7, 23** top (© Ronald van der Beek), **8** (© Vera Bogaerts), **11** (© Gary Paul Lewis), **15, 23** bottom (© SVLumagraphica), **20** (© Sebastian Duda).

Cover photograph of an iceberg reproduced with permission of istockphoto (© Erlend Kvalsvik). Back cover photograph of a woman holding a coffee cup reproduced with permission of Photolibrary (Beau Lark/Fancy).

The publishers would like to thank Nancy Harris and Adriana Scalise for their assistance in the preparation of this book.

Every effort has been made to contact copyright holders of any material reproduced in this book. Any omissions will be rectified in subsequent printings if notice is given to the publisher.

Contents

Hot materials

Some things can be hot.

Things can change when they are hot.

Hot things can be bright.

Hot things can melt.

Cold materials

Some things can be cold.

Things can change when they
are cold.

Cold things can be hard.

Cold things can be icy.

Hot and cold materials

Glass can be hot.

Glass can be bright.

Soil can be cold.
Soil can be hard.

Metal can be hot.

Metal can melt.

Metal can be cold.
Metal can be icy.

You can tell if something is hot or cold.

You can feel if something is hot
or cold.

Hot things make us feel warm.

Cold things make us feel chilly.

Cold things can get hotter.

Hot things can get colder.

Quiz

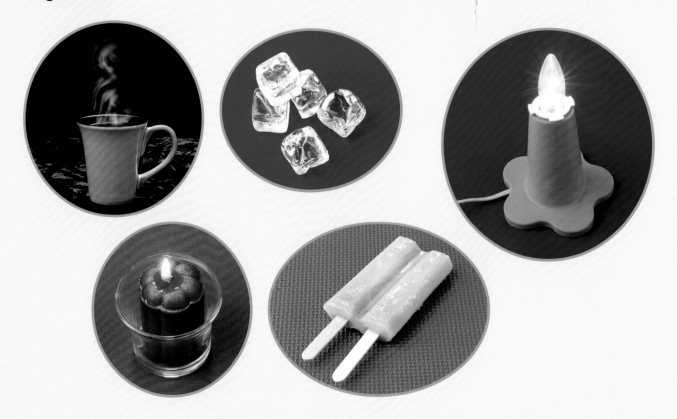

Which of these things are hot?

Which of these things are cold?

Picture glossary

melt something melts when it becomes soft and runny as it is heated

metal hard, shiny material

Index

Note to parents and teachers
Before reading
Tell children things can be hot or cold. Hot things can melt. Cold things can be icy. Ask children: "How do you know if something is hot or cold?", "Can someone give an example of something that melts?", "What is something that is icy?". Show children pictures of hot or cold things. As a class, sort the pictures into groups. As the class sorts the pictures, ask children to discuss what some of the pictures remind them of. Give children a piece of paper and tell them to fold the paper in half. Get them to draw a picture of something hot on one side and something cold on the other side.

After reading
Place children in small groups. Give each group a clear plastic cup with an ice cube in it. Ask the groups if the object in the cup is hot or cold and how they know that. Ask children to draw a picture of what the ice cube looks like as soon as they get it. Throughout the day, check on the ice cube and see how it changes over time. Each time, record what the ice cube looks like until it turns into water. Once the ice cubes melt, ask the children why they think the ice cube changed.